# MELANCHOLY DAYDREAMS

JESSICA N. CHANEY

If your life has been affected by suicide, this book is dedicated to you.

Always remember that there is an unborn life after we've died inside, and that your dreams are always possible.

# Shadow Self

My shadow self lingers
attempting to stand hand
in hand.

She copies my movements
and houses my inner rage.

**I must stay away**

Tempted by my own nightmares,
I take her hand.

My very breath bursts into
flames as I breathe.

How could I do this to *me*?

# Add Sparkle & Excitement to Any Outfit

You're like heroin in my veins, and only your
needle can break through my porcelain-
like skin to inject
your poison.

Leaving me trapped and alone in a padded room.
Causing me to fall in love with my delusions —
they keep me out of the blue.

We dance through the night under violin
skies and lie under the many moons that the
universe holds.

As we count each bedazzled gem that lines
my straight jacket.
Before drifting away back to the reality of
dreaming in my own nightmare.

Keep injecting me with your poison.
Keep flowing free.
Because of you,
my drugged
delusions are my
only sanity.

# Yes, I stole a pint glass

The woman I was before left a legacy
behind to create a new one.

Footsteps left on a path I'll never
walk again.

Memories fossilized in place with each
shoe imprint from my checkered Vans.

The feelings of living in the moment seem
surreal.

*Until I remember I have a pint glass in my pocket*

Street sides lined with bums who are able to
see straight through me.

Listening to my stories of the train I
was on being derailed, and how I'm
not able to find my way back to the
track.

Not knowing they were saving me from
myself with their kindness or how their
smiles would forever be fossilized in my
heart.

# Tap or Vodka Water?

Despite seeing my petals falling
one by one,
and feeling my thorns dry out –
easily breaking off at the stem,
roses don't know when they're dead.

So, I continue to water myself.

# The Church We Were Drunk In

Titled steeples,
prayers that are filled with lies,
under one God we fall.

# Blacksmith

You forge your own knife,
you're a blacksmith with words.
You pretend to love me,
just to make it hurt.
But I now have my own knife,
I've no need for two.
I pretend to love you,
just to give me something to do.

# I don't care, I LOVE IT

How could death be any worse?
I live in an infinity loop of pain.

Drenched in torment, I'm trapped
with no escape; when my car
went off the bridge to
meet my final fate.

It floods as if my pain were released
with black blood in the water, seeping
into the fabric of the seats.

One step closer to finding peace
as I sink to the bottom of an
abandoned city, with old brick streets.

Water fills my lungs quickly
drowning me.

But I made it to the end of life,
and oddly now, I can finally breathe.

# I Need a Hyperbaric Chamber

You're a shipwreck of emotions,
and I'm lost in your wreckage –
with my deep ocean heart so
blue.

Swells dragging me further away
from your bow.

Unwanted spirits taunting me –
RMS Republic.
Blocking me from the gold that's
said to be your heart.

Forever belonging to the sea.

# The Gallows

You stand close, never straying far.
Teaching me how to tie the knot to
my own noose.

Acting as if your touch is my savior,
and that you didn't already build the
gallows that you would graciously
lead me to.

Your lips so gently kissing mine as
you inhale my final breath.

Condemning me with what was once
perceived as true love.

# Melancholy Daydreams

Forever haunted by melancholy daydreams,
my rose bushes are bare —
exposing my picket fence fantasies.

The story of us, and how our names
are engraved on a brick at the town
four-way.

And how we were left to
crumble like the wall it once completed.

# Midwest Misery

Illinois,
please leave me alone
I'm mad.

Illinois,
you're hopeless
you hold me back.

Illinois,
you tear me apart
and cause me to sink.

Illinois,
you make me depressed
I can't even think.

Illinois,
I hate you
but I call you home.

Illinois,
why don't you love me?
I gave you my soul.

# Rest Easy

Your arms were my safe place to hide.
Now you've turned me into the definition
of dead inside.

I walk around with an inescapable feeling
of being drenched in mercury, all while
trying to breathe in a pit of lava.

The outside world has gone silent, all I
hear is my scream.
My organs lie dormant in skin that had
the most impassioned touch.

Not even the curse that was once my
inner monologue can whisper.
I jinxed myself by thinking that having
emotions was too much.

My hair drained of its red hues, as the blush
of my cheeks start to grey.

A lifetime ago my eyes were stars that
could light the darkest nights.
All I've ever wanted is love, I've
prayed.

Instead, I've been internally murdered.

The ghost of me has no eternal rest.
I'm stuck in a purgatory asylum
with murals of you painted on the
walls.

# He said…

"Have a beautiful day, cause terror."

Knowing that the only terror to cause
was within the padded walls of my mind.

My biggest fear…


**Is myself.**

# Deadly Melody

You sang your lullaby to
help me dream.

A once beautiful hymn
stuck on repeat.

And although the notes
sounded sweet, it didn't
put me to sleep.

**It killed me.**

# Powered Sugar Daydreams

A warm, full sun over the New Orleans
horizon, reflecting memories onto the
surface of the bayou that lies
below me.

Where the alligators take refuge from those
who have plans for the meat on their bones.
Poachers stalking their prey in the deep
depths of the swampy retreat.

All while I'm landing in a dark paradise...

Learning that my roots were planted with
the palm trees in the French Quarter.
Beignet after beignet, powdered sugar dreams
of a past life.

Finding beauty in the dead of the night.
In the essence of the dead witches that
linger throughout the streets outside of
Sweet Lorraine's.

Traces of dirt left on my shoes follow
me home to haunt me.
No amount of Florida water can distinguish
the good from the bad.

# Sometimes I Like Yellow

I can no longer love you
the way I do.

I'm on every page in your
coloring book, but you only
color me *blue*.

# Dear Picturesque Tragedy

If you miss me come and find me,
I'll be swimming in the deep blue abyss.

Looking for sunken ships while I wait
for an underwater kiss.

I'll swim and swim as I pretend I'm
not about to drown.

I've counted every fish I could see,
I'm still swimming around and
around.

There's no kiss to float my way,
I'm splashing, it doesn't make
a sound.

What a beautiful, picturesque tragedy
with the water so delicate, surrounding
my sheer white gown.

# Spiked Holy Water

Baptized in cyanide I've
been tainted from the start.

Every part of me dipped
except my heart.

It's poison without being
touched.

I'm cursed to feel everything,
except what it's like to be loved.

# Train 59

Finding inspiration within ourselves means
nothing without everything – the good
and the bad.
The dark, cold views of the Carbondale
sky light up the train I found my way to.

Two diamonds on a gold band with a
conductor near-by.
Small green orbs line the aisle, casting
a haze to form a path in which I must
embrace.

Taking me back to brick streets and jazz –
haunted cemeteries where I feel the most
at home.

I keep riding into the black velvet night
to find the colors within myself,
within the sunrise.
Opening gates to new journeys that I
was always meant to find.

Now the crows are cawing to me as I watch the
palms blow in the wind.
City noises as I bask in silence,
enjoying the view.

I'm allowing myself to slip into the abyss of
my mind.
Holding me captive by desire and igniting
the flame in my oil lamp.
Reminding me of what's passed and what
could have been –
where I go next and what's yet to come.

# Alone

Delusion gives me the confidence I need.
To be who I want to be.
When I'm surrounded by people
who believe in nothing.

*Someone save me.*


Or at least delude me into thinking
that I have been...

# Beauty Behind the Breakdown

His fingertips gently trace
the scars on my arm.

Leaving me feeling safe
from my own darkness.

**I am seen.**

# Love Letter in Autumn

I was set on fire like a love
letter that would never be
read.

He watched my ashes fall
and drift through the autumn
breeze.

Twirling and dancing with the
warm colors of the wind.

Little does he know, he only
set me free.

# Rain Rain Don't Go Away

I love the falling rain,
it brings me back to life.

The sky's an endless grey,
drained of sunlight.

For many others, the Sun's a
sign of life.

But for me, dreary skies are
just right.

# The Letter K

You expect me to wear
your initial around my neck,
while you remain unsure if
you can love me...


**K.**

# The Chair

I'm trying to convince myself to keep the
clothes in my room off of the chair.

'Come on Jessica. We have hangers for a reason.'

For an organized woman, I really surprise
myself at how much I hate putting laundry
away.

The chair is close... I can easily grab what I
need and gather different outfit ideas while it
all lies in front of me.

*Visualization*

Future fashion designer? Definitely not.

I suppose my bedroom can often be a
reflection of my mind since it is my only
place away from others.

Where I can lie in the dark and listen
to violin while basking in my melancholy
daydreams...

...with the clothes still left on the chair.
The same way my thoughts purge my
mind – in a cluster and mostly at once.

Maybe I will try to rearrange my thoughts
as I hang up each shirt that's forgotten what
a closet looks like –

Organized and free from being suffocated by
the others that have been piled on top.

# 30

Degenerate beauty queen,
I was longing to be seen.
Nothing left of me except tear
drops in my sheets – how could
you do this to me?
Now, I'm too far gone to ever
feel a thing.

# Small Town Blues

Living in a small town, I can never hide.
Crippling anxiety keeps me inside.
Surrounded by people who think they
know me... who they know is me when
I was 19.

I don't know what to do, I feel so alone.
Been pushed so far that now I rarely
answer the phone.

Who is it? This person I've become.
I keep to myself; I've given up on love.

My dreams use to sparkle and shine.
Now my dreams consist of Cracklin'
Cranberry, the seasonal wine.

I wanted white roses and a black picket
fence.
A traditional love that's sustainable, that
makes sense.

Inside of me I die a little more each day.
Stuck in a small Midwest town where
everyone knows my name.

I'm a prisoner here, and the death of me
it will be.

Stuck in a small town, I've said goodbye
to my dreams.

# Overruled

The blue dragon and the
castle in the park – you made
me feel alive, I felt the spark.

We explored the tunnels of
the castle together – the air was
cold but it didn't matter.

In those moments, I felt alive.
A queen on the throne with a
king by her side.

But life took an unexpected turn…

Fires started, and the castle bridge
was burned.

You left me to be trapped with no
way out.

The mote was destroyed by you,
without a doubt.

Your intentions quickly became
clear.
Your plan was to rule my kingdom,
but you live in fear.

Fear that you could never truly be a
ruler to a kingdom in need.

You thought you trapped me inside,
but the reign belongs to me.

# Vulnerable

I leave the curtains open
while I bathe.

The setting sun beams onto
my pale skin.

I am my most vulnerable self
for all to see.

# Devil's Mistress

I'm famously lovable –
that's what my horoscope said.

But I'm only famous when shitty
men want me in their beds.

It feels like I was meant to be
the other woman – no wedding
dress or veil.

Just me and my demons, wishing
me well.

They're all I have to tuck me in
at night.
But am I safe from them when I
turn off the lights?

They conquer my brain as if it were a
war to be won.
They hold me close and never let
me run.

It turns out my mind is a fucked up
place to be.

A combination of a battlefield and a
wet dream.

Maybe a Tim Burton movie...
or a horror scene.

Even still, I can feel the rapture growing
inside of me – with the urge to yell and
set fire to the streets.

The price of living is agonizing heartbreak,
even when I'm a lover every day.

The pain flows through my veins like a
lethal injection, waiting for my eyes to close.

Love is no longer an option.

*Follow our commands, maybe we'll let you go.*

# Into the Unknown

There were many nights I prayed
that you would die.

I spent years giving love
when you were never by my side.

As you put your gun in my mouth,
telling me to open wide.

But I let you do it —
so, is it murder or suicide?

I loved you too much,
never seeing the darkness
behind your eyes.

Now that the darkness has
faded, shades of amber shine.

This time around things feel
different.
Can we become the
Great Divine?

I now hold your heart in my hands,
while you beg to hold mine.

I wonder if things could be better,
could this be the perfect time?

Can I hand over my heart?
Are we finding love in summertime?

What would happen to it if I did?
Would you cherish it or say goodbye?

I love you too much to not give
love a try.

The truth is that I'll love you forever
but I fear the unknown.

I'm scared to give you my heart,
but what's the worst that can happen
to stone?

# Clorox On the Rocks

Keep taking your love away,
never give it back.

You dropped my heart on the
ground, put it in a body bag.

Internal death, no one to
resurrect.

My mind's a haunted mansion
with ghosts of the past.

Sticks and stones and grass
that's not green, stuck in
purgatory, I drank the holy
water but should have drunk
the bleach.

# Fire Proximity Suit

I'm not interested in the lies you
keep spouting.
Echoing through the meadow of
my mind.
Causing the meadow to burst into
flames, spreading like the California
wildfires.
Making my mind turn into a cloud of
smokey ash.

Hazardous love is the most painful
thing I've ever felt in my life.
I've had every part of me completely
demolished.

Making me hate my life, hate myself,
and everything around me.

And then have been healed by the same
person who caused the pain.

Still burning for them.
Looking at them and hating them, but
wanting nothing more than to feel the
touch of their lips on mine, and to be
in their arms.

Love is anguish.
It's pure and utter disgust.
So why do I keep going back and
chasing it?
Knowing it will lead me to my grave,
not being able to give up or let go.

May our hearts forever be set ablaze,
and then frozen in time together,
for eternity.

# Empty Locket

During my impending doom,
I still imagine being a ballerina.

Dancing with a hollow heart and
grace.

Rose petals falling while I listen
to the colors of the piano.

No pink tutu but emerald green
satin.
My hair down and in loose curls.

Dancing in a dark paradise by
the ocean – where there's always
a chill breeze, and the sun never shines.

The only light I have to guide me
reflects onto my locket from the
moonlight.

I am alone at midnight and mid-day,
waiting for someone to watch me dance.

# Roses Die

Do you remember that night?
Two bouquets after the fight.

The story of a girl – go ahead
and drown the whole world.

*Daft peasant whore –*
*can't you see that I don't love*
*you anymore?*

You told me to drink and drive.
*Anything is better than you staying*
*alive.*

You looked at me with so much hate.
As I sat on the bed shocked, not
knowing what to say.

I sat in silence after you left.
My heart shattered on the bed.

I packed my bags and was ready
to leave.
Until you pulled into the drive-way,
threatening me not to flee.

*I hate you, I love you*, you said as
my soul bursts into flames.

My ashes floated through the midnight
sky, more still than the world when it rains.

Like a tumbleweed, I drifted far.
You said drink and drive, so I got in my car.
Barely able to hold the wheel as
tears filled my eyes, it should have

been the last time we said goodbye.

I was thinking about forever, trying to
keep the spark alive.

You had a group of girls kept to the side.

Was it ever love?
Or was it in my head?

Maybe you were right...
I'm better off dead.

# Suicidal at Best

My heart of gold means nothing anymore.
I'd rather be tied up, bleeding out on
the kitchen floor.

I could die tomorrow, and no one would
be fazed.

I should have died that night in December,
still a Christmas day.

Blood spurting from my arm,
and the ambulance far away –
I was friends with the cops, they
didn't know what to say.

With tears falling from their eyes, Blake
held my hand when I asked if this was
goodbye.

I remember feeling frozen, like an ice
queen.
No blood in my body, my mind diminishing.

I knew I was about to die, but something
kept me from closing my eyes.

The pain can be overbearing.
I wish I could explain the feeling in my chest –
sinking but numb, my body feels like it's
drowning in quicksand.

I'm always an option, never the girl chosen first.
At least at this point, love can no longer hurt.

I give my whole heart and still come in last.
Now I listen to the ghosts talking, telling
me to **do it again**.

# Liquid Lungs

All life does is kill me.
You'd figure that after being lost
in the sea for so long that I would
have turned into a mermaid by now.

Or at least know how to swim…

I feel like Stefan when he's locked in
the safe at the bottom of the quarry —
every time he wakes up, he drowns
all over again.

While everyone goes on with their lives
not knowing how bad the suffering
<u>actually</u> is.

# Hershey's Kiss

Last time I saw you
was our sweetest goodbye.

Melting chocolate on a hot
summer day.

Melted and forever changed,
but better than before.

# Have you tried Gorilla Glue?

The foundation of my heart has cracked.

And although it may look beautiful,
Victorian even, it must be evacuated
before it collapses.

Holding you captive and *hoping* that
you can reconstruct what's deemed
to be beyond repair.

# Fruit and Honey

Fresh fruit and sugar scents in the air —
dripping honey feels freeing,
life **finally** seems fair.

# Aberdeen

I left my heart in the cold streets of Aberdeen
for you to find.
You were gone to sea
and I was desperate to feel you with me.

Exploring the dark side streets by the harbor,
I was hoping you would appear.

*Pint glasses of Tennent's*
*Frankie in a gas mask*
*The power of your smile*

I was looking for you in fading faces
but you were gone.

All I wanted was to dance with you
in the castle.
To sneak away so we could be lost
in each other,
and to see how our different worlds would
collide.

I left it there...
my heart.

In hopes that you would find it and keep it safe,
but a pirate appeared and took it deep into the
North Sea where it still floats aimlessly.

Waiting for your hands to grab ahold of it and
bring it back to the stone streets by the harbor.
But it was lost, and you stopped looking.

# <u>Author's note:</u>

As a suicide survivor, I understand what it means to feel like there is no beauty after dying inside.

I hope that this book can help you feel that you are not alone, and that beauty can come from sadness.

If you are struggling to love life, or just waking up every day, I want you to make this book not only mine, but yours.

Write about it – even if you feel that it doesn't make much sense in the moment.

I encourage you to sit with those negative feelings, and to embrace them, because in the end, it turns into something beautiful.


Never stop moving forward.

"What if someone had asked Picasso not to be sad?
Never known who he was, or the man he'd become
There would be no Blue Period.
Let me run with the wolves, let me do what I do.
Let me show you how sadness can turn into happiness,
I can turn blue into something beautiful."

-Lana Del Rey

Who inspires you to be your best self?

_____

_____

_____

_____

_____

_____

_____

_____

_____

_____

_____

_____

_____

_____

_____

What are three things you value about yourself?

_____

_____

_____

_____

_____

_____

_____

_____

_____

_____

_____

_____

_____

_____

_____

_____

What is something you need to forgive yourself for?

_____

_____

_____

_____

_____

_____

_____

_____

_____

_____

_____

_____

_____

_____

_____

How does forgiveness impact your emotions?

_____

_____

_____

_____

_____

_____

_____

_____

_____

_____

_____

_____

_____

_____

_____

_____

What is a painful memory that you hold onto? How can you
accept the pain and move forward?

_____

_____

_____

_____

_____

_____

_____

_____

_____

_____

_____

_____

_____

_____

What is one belief about yourself that ties you to emotional pain?
What can you do to let that belief go?

_____

_____

_____

_____

_____

_____

_____

_____

_____

_____

_____

_____

_____

_____

_____

_____

What is a dream that you would like to accomplish?

_____

_____

_____

_____

_____

_____

_____

_____

_____

_____

_____

_____

_____

_____

What makes you resilient?

What are steps that you can take to improve communicating
negative emotions?

_____

_____

_____

_____

_____

_____

_____

_____

_____

_____

_____

_____

_____

_____

What perspectives can you adopt to help ease negative triggers?

_____

_____

_____

_____

_____

_____

_____

_____

_____

_____

_____

_____

_____

_____

_____

# About the Author

Jessica Chaney is from a small town in Southern Illinois. She graduated from Saint Louis University with a degree in Emergency Management and currently works as a Regional Planner, with a background in EMS/Disaster Preparedness.

Throughout her life, Jessica has struggled to process the strong emotions of pain she has often faced. Before writing, she resorted to alcohol abuse as a form of coping that only left her with more pain, until she discovered the healing power of poetry – which led to her first anthology of poems, *Melancholy Daydreams*.

Her goal with sharing her writing is to show others who may be suffering, that life can move forward, and that they are not alone.

www.ingramcontent.com/pod-product-compliance
Lightning Source LLC
Chambersburg PA
CBHW041628140626
46547CB00031B/1179